Mel Bay Presents

The TITANIC Songbook

Music As Heard On The Fateful Voyage — April 1912

A Collection By Ian Whitcomb
Edited by Ronny S. Schiff
Compilation and Essay by Ian Whitcomb

A full recording of this music
Ian Whitcomb's *Titanic – Music As Heard On The Fateful Voyage* (R#72821)
produced by Rhino Records,
is available at your local music store or by calling 800-432-0020.

Visit us on the Web at http://www.melbay.com — E-mail us at email@melbay.com

ABOUT THE AUTHOR

Ian Whitcomb, born in England in 1941, has performed popular songs since childhood. At prep school, he organized a comb-and-tissue paper band to play such current hits as "Answer Me" and "Shrimp Boats"; at boarding school he introduced his version of rock 'n' roll. In his late teens, he discovered ragtime and rhythm & blues. While he was a history major at Trinity College, Dublin, in the early 1960s, he studied, wrote about, and played American pop. By chance, his recording of a novelty song he'd made up, "You Turn Me On," shot him into the American Top Ten in 1965.

As a rock star, Whitcomb toured with the Rolling Stones and the Beach Boys, but his interest in the roots of pop, especially ragtime and Tin Pan Alley, caused him to neglect his teen idol career and to concentrate on researching and performing this largely forgotten music.

The result has been a flow of books, records, documentaries, radio shows, and concerts. He has played everywhere, from the Hollywood Bowl and the Montreux Jazz Festival to shopping malls and private homes. He has contributed, on record and sheet music, his own rags and songs in the grand old Alley tradition. He was even allowed to perform on "The Tonight Show," "Today," and "Tom Snyder." For over a decade, he has been spreading the "word" in Southern California via his radio show on NPR affiliate stations. He lives near the mountains in Altadena, California with his singing wife Regina.

BOOKS BY IAN WHITCOMB

After the Ball: Pop Music from Rag to Rock (1972)

Tin Pan Alley: A Pictorial History (1975)

Lotusland A Story of Southern California (1979)

Whole Lotta Shakin': A Rock 'n' Roll Scrapbook (1982)

Rock Odyssey: A Chronicle of the Sixties (1983)

Irving Berlin & Ragtime America (1987)

Resident Alien (1990)

The Beckoning Fairground: Notes of a British Exile (1994)

Treasures of Tin Pan Alley (1994, Mel Bay Publications, Inc.)

Vaudeville Favorites (1995, Mel Bay Publications, Inc.)

The Best Of Vintage Dance (1996, Mel Bay Publications, Inc.)

Songs of the Ragtime Era (1997, Mel Bay Publications, Inc.)

Contents In Order of Appearance in the Book

Table of Contents

TITANIC

Heroes of Light Music —

[TESTIMONY OF TWO *TITANIC* SURVIVORS]

From aft came the tunes of the band. It was a ragtime tune – I don't know what. Then there was 'Autumn'... The way the band kept playing was a noble thing... The last I saw of the band, when I was floating out to sea with my life belt on, it was still playing 'Autumn.' How they ever did it I cannot imagine.

– Harold Bride, Marconi wire operator

Many brave things were done that night but none more brave than by those few men playing minute after minute as the ship settled quietly lower and lower in the sea and the sea rose higher and higher to where they stood – the music they played serving alike as their own immortal requiem and their right to be recorded on the rolls of undying fame.

– Lawrence Beesley, Dulwich College schoolmaster

The White Star Orchestra

[original]

Fred Clark OF LIVERPOOL • **Percy Taylor** OF CLAPHAM

G. Krins OF BRIXTON • **Wallace Hartley** OF DEWSBURY • **Ted Brailey** OF NOTTING HILL

Jock Hume OF DUMFRIES • **George Woodward** OF HEADINGTON, OXON

NOT PICTURED **Roger Bricoux** OF LILLE

The little girl lay dying in a room at the Salvation Army mission in Kirkcudbright, Scotland. The officer in charge was summoned. "Captain," she said, "Hold my hand – I am so afraid. Can't you see that big ship sinking? Look at all those people drowning. Someone called Wally is playing a fiddle and coming at you."

The captain looked around and saw nobody. But then he heard the downstairs door click open, and when he went to investigate he felt someone whisk past him, briny-wet. The captain leapt upstairs again and into the little girl's room. "Mother has come to take me to heaven," she said. Then she died, and the captain heard the downstairs door latch click once more. When telling his tale he added: "Some hours later the whole world was startled by the tragedy of the Titanic. Among those drowned was Wally Hartley, whom I knew well as a boy. I had no knowledge of his going to sea or having anything to do with any ship."

On that night of April 14, 1912, in a few seconds of legendary hubris, the unsinkable collided with the unthinkable, and the first lesson of the twentieth century began.

R.M.S. *Titanic,* pride of the White Star line, had been cleaving a calm but icy Atlantic on her maiden voyage from Southampton to New York. Wireless messages warned of "bergs, growlers, and field ice." The lookout men had no binoculars. There were life-boats for just over half of the 2,208 people aboard, more than the regulations demanded. The ship could stay afloat easily with two of her watertight compartments flooded. She could even survive with up to four breached.

¶ At 11:40 p.m. the gilded palace – triple-screwed, four-funneled, steam-powered, electrically lit, and with electric elevators and an electric organ – the last word in luxury liners, and the largest man-made floating object in the world, sideswiped an enormous iceberg. This ill-designed and malodorous object concealed beneath its waterline crooked fingers of ice, all hard as rocks and steely sharp.

¶ And as the floating Xanadu blazed past the black mass (hoping to avoid a meeting), the deadly fingers tore into her starboard hull, creating six thin slits in an area no bigger than two squares of pavement. But that was enough to expose a contained and comfortable Edwardian civilization to the water cannon fire of an unstoppable ocean. Six watertight compartments were ready for flooding. The great ship was doomed.

¶ At 2:20 a.m. on April 15 the ship, broken in two and with its rear upended rudely, took its nosedive. There was a gurgling, then silence, followed by a steady, heavy moan. This chorus of the dying lasted an hour.

¶ Sent to the ocean floor were thousands of pounds of poultry and game, sausages and sweetbreads, a set of bagpipes, a marmalade machine, and seven parcels of parchment of the Hebrew Holy Scrolls. Also, five grand pianos and two uprights (for steerage class singalongs). True to chivalrous Anglo-Saxon tradition, great efforts were made to get the women and children into the lifeboats first. Next came the first-class passengers. Too many third-class passengers had waited sheepishly in their lower deck accommodations, assuming their place in the lower rungs of society. There was never any real panic. It was all so unexpected.

¶ Some 1,500 people died, mostly from exposure, 705 were rescued. The funeral ship picked up corpses bobbing about in life belts and a frozen tableau of an old gentleman in full evening dress holding aloft a tiny child. Another retrieved body was that of the ship's bandmaster, Wallace Hartley. His violin case was strapped to his chest. All eight members of his orchestra perished with him.

¶ Legend, instantly created by the newspapers in order to give readers what they needed (which was legend, full of old-time chivalry), has it that the brave little band steadfastly played right on till the very end, even when the ship's stern was tipped up. And, according to legend, as the waters enclosed, it was playing the hymn "Nearer My God To Thee."

¶ While, in the aftermath, blame fell on many of the players in the *Titanic* tragedy, the reputation of her musicians soared heavenward, fashioning them into folk heroes. They were honored with more memorials than any of the famous names who died in the disaster: with plaques in New York, Boston, and Liverpool; and a concert at London's Albert Hall, at which celebrated composer Sir Edward Elgar acted as conductor-in-chief, presided over 7 orchestras and 500 performers. Up to 30,000 mourners attended the funeral of bandmaster Wallace Hartley at Colne, his birthplace in Lancashire. Professional musicians traveled from all over the British Isles to pay their respects to a noble member of their company, one who had died in harness, on the job, at the gig.

¶ But as far as the White Star Line was concerned this was simply a case of business as usual. No compensation was offered to the bereaved families of the musicians. Nor were the musicians' agents any more charitable: violinist Jock Hume's father was sent a bill for his lost uniform ("Lyre lapel insignia – 2 shillings; sewing of White Star buttons on tunic – 1 shilling"). Finally, in 1913, "The Titanic Relief Fund" came to the rescue, deciding that the bandsmen were all members of the crew and therefore entitled to remuneration – for the parsimonious White Star Line had taken the musicians aboard as second-class passengers in order to avoid paying union rates.

¶ That the band was treated so shabbily by their employers was typical of the relationship between master and servant in those days. Musicians – unless they were celebrities – were merely functionaries, and therefore they came to the ball through the back door, the servant's entrance.

¶ That the *Titanic* band's music is still remembered, still performed, and still gives pleasure – while most of their contemporary "betters" are forgotten – is testimony not only to their heroism but also to the emotional power of music, and in particular to the popular music of their times. The Edwardians enjoyed a cornucopia of musical styles that knew no barriers, provided such music was present in the right place and at the right time. Good manners were everything. You never violated the peace of others. You didn't whistle at breakfast; you tipped the organ-grinder under your window so as to make him move along; you held the key that unlocked the piano.

¶ And the British Isles were filled with music – from grand opera and symphonic concerts to brass band contests between rival factories and coal mines; from rude and racy music hall songs to genteel drawing room ballads. No home was complete without a piano, however cloaked, however trousered. Young men took their banjos to parties, while maidens, armed with a bound book of music, hoped to win a husband with the sweetness of a sentimental song.

¶ All this music, great or humble, was popular. There was, as yet, no distinction between high-brow and lowbrow. Organ-grinders played Brahms and Bizet and Wagner. Sir Edward Elgar wrote popular waltzes. Classically trained musicians wrote for the frothy, girlie-filled musical comedies. Music hall songs could please royal ears: Queen Victoria had been fond of a piece called "Come Where The Booze Is Cheaper." General Booth of the Salvation Army wished to God that his people could come up with tunes as catchy.

¶ This was a golden age of music in Britain – and much was British-made, yet soon twilight would pervade, because American ragtime was cantering in. Night fell with the coming of jazz just after the Great War: the friendly invasion. But in the Edwardian age Britain led the field in the exploitation and acceptance of popular music. Though it's been called "light" and not "serious," the best is full of delight, producing the kind of tingling shudder one gets from the first spoonful of a really delicious dessert. The making of such confections required many years of study. Melody must be made to undulate prettily atop a crust of rich harmony. The whole affair came together in one magnificent ornamental pie when the music was set before the public for atmosphere only – for performance from behind the potted palm, when the band, usually a string ensemble, was but an amenity of the hotel, tea room, cafe, or ocean liner.

¶ Then, and only then, could a bandleader offer up a mixture of opera, overture, suite, fantasie, caprice, idyll, intermezzo and sprinkle it with some notes from a march, music hall ditty, or latest hit from the musical comedy stage. Perhaps, by 1911, a little ragtime pepper could be judiciously applied. Good taste – that was the secret. Singing was not on the menu. Dancing was discouraged.

¶ The band – or "orchestra" if you wanted pretension – was to play discreetly from behind the potted palm (hence the term *Palm Court music).* The huge music library (352 tunes listed in White Star's book) had to be learned by heart and known by number. (That's why even today songs are referred to as "numbers.") However, the great point to remember was to never draw attention to yourself. "Don't forget lads," said Hartley as they boarded the great ship on Wednesday, April 10 at Southampton, "we're in the service trade. We're servants playing in the minstrel gallery."

¶ Hartley was proud of his boys; he handpicked them himself. The agency be damned. Those Scrooges up in Liverpool. These boys had experience from the school of hard knocks – from theater pit orchestras and music halls, from grand hotels and dim cafes, but all had solid classical training. Monsieur Roger Bricoux was a Continental gentleman and thus perfect for the Gallic authenticity needed at the ship's Café Parisien. Bricoux would be part of the trio playing outside the café, while Hartley lead the main group, the quintet, in the first-class lounge, second-class lounge, and the dining room, and, of course, at teatime.

¶ Sometimes all eight musicians would split up into other configurations and go strolling from room to room, from table to table. Now *that* could lead to some good tips, but one must be ready to play requests. Very important that. Young Jock Hume was a past master at the request game. Such a merry and bright lad from Scotland, not a bit dour. A terrific busker – could play anything so long as you hum him a few bars. Recently a wealthy Yankee fellow requested "something classy and classical." So Jock took one of those new ragtime numbers but played it dead slow and stately. The Yankee was so impressed. Gave Jock a big tip and a slap on the back.

¶ **Wallace Henry Hartley was born in Colne, Lancashire, in 1878. As a boy chorister he'd sung under the baton of his father, choirmaster at the local Bethel Methodist church. Wallace learned to love the hymns for their soaring majesty and sense of certainty. The tunes marched valiantly, always to a firm step. "Eternal Father, Strong To Save" made him crave the sea. "Nearer, My God To Thee" awed and frightened him. An exciting mix.**

¶ By January 1912, at the ripe old age of 33, Wallace Hartley, a fully professional all-round musician, was doing quite nicely. A skilled violinist (and a nimble fiddler for the jigs, reels, and ragtime) and something of a composer, he was also an able and amiable orchestra leader. Recently he'd made cruise ships his specialty. Cunard had just employed him as bandmaster on their *Mauretania*, and now those pushy White Star people were at him again to lead an ensemble – this time on their latest luxury liner.

¶   He had a reputation as a well-trained musician who was blessed with the common touch. Well, not too common – seeing as how the clientele were mostly snobs or, at least, *nouveau riche*. Anyway, Wallace knew hundreds of numbers by memory, and he also held views about the use of music as medicine. Nice medicine, a decent tonic to give you a fillip. A few months ago, while serving as bandmaster on the *Celtic,* he'd been asked by a journalist how he'd cope in a nautical calamity. "Why, you know," he replied, adding his famous crooked smile, "I've always felt that when men are called upon to face death suddenly, music is far more effective in cheering them on than all the firearms in creation. Should an accident befall my ship I know that every one of the men would stick with me and play until the waters engulfed us." Fine, but what sort of music? "Lively stuff, of course. None of your hymns, although I dearly love them. My favorite is 'Nearer My God To Thee' – but I'm keeping that one reserved for my funeral." And he added a chuckle.

I led my loyal lads to their unnumbered cabin on E Deck. Rather cramped quarters, near the stern, and right next door to the noisy potato washing machine. Ship's bandsmen can't be choosers – and you got good eats and good tips, with the right attitude, of course.

We have very attractive uniforms. Lots of them: blue jackets and white jackets and jackets with green facings and fancy piping – all for separate occasions and locations, and all paid for out of our pockets. I'd spoken to Mr. J. Bruce Ismay, the White Star boss, about this hardship and others, but Mr. Ismay was unmovable. Still, the boss is going to be a passenger on the maiden voyage, so maybe there'll be a chance to get his ear during the trip. I know he's partial to musical comedy and, in particular, to the fetching daintiness of Gertie Millar, especially when she skips around the stage singing "Moonstruck" with that line, "I'm such a silly when the moon comes out." A lot of middle-aged gentlemen develop rapid pulses when Miss Millar cavorts. She's the ideal mistress. There'll be a lot of mistresses aboard this ship, I'll wager – under the usual assumed names. I know that, you see, because there's a lot of millionaires registered. I hear that J.P. Morgan, the American multimillionaire and the real owner of this ship and whole bally White Star Line, has canceled his stateroom at the last minute. I wonder why. This is going to be a really tip-top gala voyage – and our job is very important.

On with the job! We'll have Ted Brailey start off the proceedings by playing "The White Star March" on the brand new Aeolian electric organ in the First Class lounge. That should put them in a bright mood. After that it's all go – we're scheduled to play in the Palm Court and the Verandah and the lounge and the dining room. This calls for elegant selections as befitting a ship appointed with rich carpets, polished oak, velvet curtains, original oil paintings, Jacobean designs, Greek pillars, and I know not what...so we'll perform numbers like the aria from Samson And Delilah and probably some Elgar. What a way with a melody! In between the romantic stuff we'll stick some perkiness – "Glow-Worm," from the German operetta Lysistrata, a nice little idyll, which means a poem in pastoral style. These descriptive pieces are awfully effective, giving quiet pleasure and no disturbance to conversation. People can enjoy their drinks and play their card games. Even build card houses – they say this ship is so stable there'll be no rocking. If we had a proper dance floor people could jig away without bumping into each other like on some of those cheap cruises. Of course, I've no doubt there will be some ad hoc dancing, especially when we play ragtime, all the rage at present, even in England. They say every tune is written by one little fellow called Irving Berlin, a Yank who can't read or write a note of music. Whatever next! And the titles they dream up, these Yanks! Referring to women as "Beautiful Dolls" and "Honey Babes." The ragtime is certainly giving our native writers a run for their money. But Lionel Monckton and Leslie Stuart can more than hold their own against the invaders, turning out equally fast trot music and, of course, their trademark lilting tunes. At dinner we'll play selections from Monckton's The Arcadians, another hit musical comedy full of girlie girls with curly curls. Whimsy, pure whimsy. And charm, so much charm!

But the ragtime seems to be the theme sound of our new century. We keep getting requests for numbers about odd American spots. The Wild West and the Deep South, etc. Exciting goings-on down on the levée in old Alabammy, waitin' fer the Robert E. Lee... What a drive the song has! Still, we'll leave the Robert E. Lee till after dinner, when the passengers are loosened up, a bit lubricated, and messing about in the lounge. Besides, during dinner there's such an ocean storm of chatter and clatter that we have a hard job being heard at all. That's when we can perform Britain's own contribution to the romance of the American West. That's when we can play "Lily of Laguna" by our very own Leslie Stuart. He's never been near Laguna, which is, I believe, on the coast of California. No, Stuart located the sweet-flowing name on a map. I know him and he's a grand fellow, all hail-fellow-well-met, a Lancashire lad like me who used to be an organist at the Catholic cathedral in Salford. Real name's Tommy Barrett. He writes a really rolling melody, and the modulations in "Lily" are so clever. Spends far too much time at the race course, though, and is on overly friendly terms with the bottle.

There's no need to live the bohemian life. Take another of our native composers, Archibald Joyce, who wrote the jewel of a waltz we like to finish off the evening with: "Songe d'Automne" – how they love those classy French titles! Joyce is a different kettle of fish compared to poor old Tommy B. Again, I know him – a tight little band are we pro musicians – and we're both composers and bandmasters on cruise ships. He's only a few years older than me, but he's a long way ahead in terms of career. Plays violin and piano, but likes to conduct from the keyboard. Got the market cornered on the posh gigs to be sure. His bands and orchestras are in demand at all the high-class affairs – stately home balls, hunt balls, Oxford and Cambridge balls, you name it. He's the dance leader par excellence, and that's all he's happy doing: working for dancers. We call him the English Waltz King. He's made a contribution by slowing down the whirling, dizzying European waltz to a dreamy pace much loved by courting couples. With his pince-nez and his trim mustache he cuts an imperious figure on the bandstand – his father was a Grenadier Guards band sergeant – but he's really quite a cuddly sort, and he's very particular about paying attention to the right rhythms for his beloved dancers. To me Archibald Joyce is a model bandmaster. And he can write the Yank stuff too. He's written some cakewalks and rags. There's no secret to it...

Around 11 p.m. we can knock off, unless the requests are really lucrative, and retire to our bandroom for a chin-wag, a smoke, and a bit of a tipple.

Sunday morning and all's well, flat as a millpond on the ocean. We all played for the morning Divine Service, conducted by Captain Smith, who certainly looks the part, all beard and noble bearing. Among the hymns was my thrilling "Eternal Father, Strong To Save." Afterwards, between gigs, I sneaked down to steerage with Percy Taylor, one of our pianists. Percy had begged me to come and hear some American vaudeville act called The Musical Murrays who've been amusing the poorer passengers. Apparently the American act got stranded in Scotland due to a music hall manager not coughing up their cash. The act's stage slogan is very funny: "Not The Best But As Good As The Rest." Well, I found them top-hole – lots of banjo, xylophone, and even an accordion. They did a rollicking song about a Frankie and Johnny, very different to our way of playing. A certain swing. The boys have learned some of our music hall tunes, and they proudly showed them off to us, while the steerage passengers danced and carried on.

I could have stayed down there all day so infectious was the music. But time was getting on and I told Percy we'd better be nipping along back to the first-class lounge where we'd left Ted Brailey keeping the clientele happy with sentimental ballads like "Somewhere A Voice Is Calling" played with all stops out on the

electric organ. We relieved him and settled into "In The Shadows," a dainty dance by fellow bandleader Herman Finck, who's done a lot to improve the sound of London's pit orchestras. Syd Baynes, another fine conductor, slipped me an arrangement of his latest waltz just before I left London for this gig: "Destiny" – what a catchy set of melodies! Sure to be a hit – we played it at lunch, got requests at teatime, and we'll play it again tonight...

Our last time together...there's not much to say about the official music we played tonight. We played a recital after dinner and knocked off around 11 p.m., heading for the band room for a smoke and a natter. About half an hour later we were disturbed by a shudder followed by a sort of grinding noise. Probably the potato washing machine working overtime, George Krins said, always the jokester. Then, a little later, one of the stewarts popped in to tell us we'd hit an iceberg, quite unthinkable, and that the lifeboats were being lowered.

I knew what to do. I've always been ready for such an occasion. I told the lads to get back into their uniforms and follow me to A Deck. We'd set up in the lounge and play an ad hoc set. Lively tunes, nothing morbid. Ragtime would certainly fit the bill. There mustn't be any panic. Nor was anybody panicking as far as I could see. The passengers, some in night clothes, some in evening dress, were milling about – chatting, joking, smoking. The bar was open and the drinks were on the house. A group of gents were playing cards rather seriously. There were an awful lot of dogs.

People pretended to ignore our music, but I think it was helpful. At least, I like to think so. They all seemed so cheerful. As the ship sank lower we moved higher, up to the grand staircase, the one with all the blazing lights and the impressive dome. What can I say? We played away and they all processed passed us. One toff even threw down a tip, a great wad of banknotes. We never thought twice about it. We were just doing our job.

Eventually, toward the end, we went outside onto the deck itself, just me and the strings. I must say it was bitterly cold and we had no gloves. I announced that we might as well play #114, "Songe d'Automne," the tune we usually wind up the evening with by dear old Archie Joyce. Sounded a trifle gloomy, under the circumstances, but it's so beautiful and the sea was so calm and all the stars were out. Even though there must have been lots of noise and what have you around us, I wasn't aware. In fact, I became less and less aware of my surroundings, of the situation. I let myself climb up the stairs and step inside the music itself, right snug between the blankets of harmony, caught in a juicy chord. Then we took off for home and I was remembering my childhood in Lancashire and the first time I discovered the thrill of music, how it lifts you up and over the hills and far away so that eventually you forget everything except a thick essence of vibration, an endless, whirling song which, nevertheless, is at the center quite still.

– Ian Whitcomb

THE
WHITE STAR
POLKA-MARCH
BY
J.T. GARDNER.

Copyright. · LONDON · FRANCIS · DAY & HUNTER · late FRANCIS BROS & DAY Blenheim House · 195 · OXFORD St · W
Publishers of Smallwood's Celebrated Tutor. The Easiest to Teach and to Learn From.

Price 4/-
Septett 1/- Nett.
Full Orchestra 1/6 ··

The White Star March

By J.T. Gardner

Arr. Linda M. Cummings

Last time to Coda

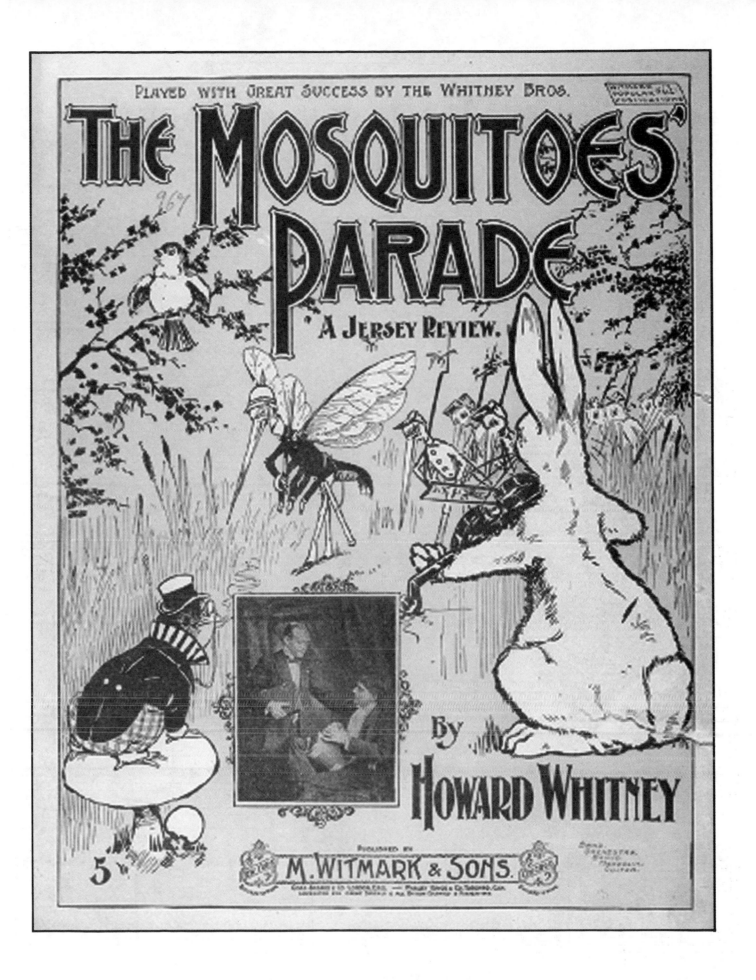

"THE MOSQUITOS' PARADE."

(A JERSEY REVIEW.)

By HOWARD WHITNEY.
(OF WHITNEY BROTHERS.)

THE MOSQUITOS' PARADE

21

TRIO.

22

Mon cœur s'ouvre à ta voix

from
SAMSON ET DALILA

Camille Saint-Saëns

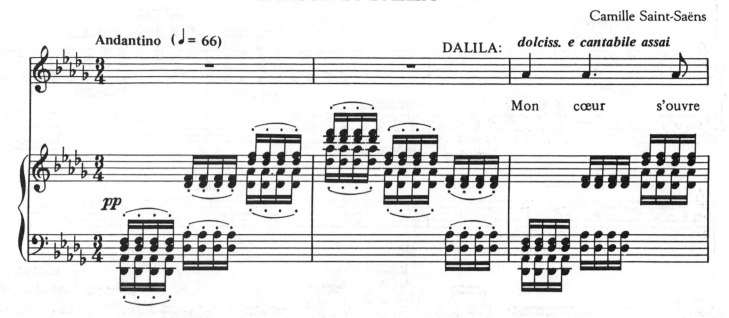

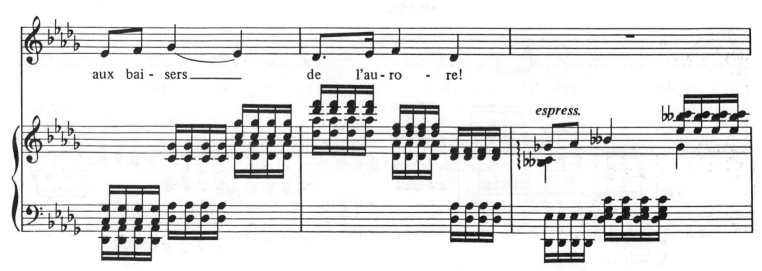

Mais, ô mon bien-ai-mé,
pour mieux sé-cher mes pleurs, que ta voix parle en-co-re!
Dis-moi qu'à Da-li-la tu re-viens pour ja-

dim.

pp

rinf.

sf *p* *pp*

mais; re - dis à ma ten - dres - se les ser -

ments d'au - tre - fois — ces ser - ments que j'ai -

mais! Ah! ré -

ponds à ma ten - dres - se!

Ver - se moi,_____ ver-se-moi_____ l'i-

vres - se! Ré - ponds____ à ma ten-dres - se!

senza accel.
cresc.

più cresc.

Ré - ponds____ à ma ten-dres - se! Ah!_____ Ver-se-

f

cresc.

moi,_____ ver-se-moi_____ l'i - vres - se!

dim.

p

pp

ain - si fré - mit mon cœur,

prêt à se con - so - ler _____

à ta voix _____ qui m'est chè - re!

rinf.

La

poco animato

flè - che est moins ra - pide   à por -

ter   le   tré - pas   que ne

l'ést _____ ton a - man - te à vo -

29

moi_____ l'i - vres - se! Ré - ponds___ à ma ten-

dres - se! Ré - ponds___ à ma ten - dres - se! Ah!_____ Ver - se -

moi,_____ ver - se - moi_____ l'i - vres - se! Sam-son!

Sam-son! je___ t'ai - me!

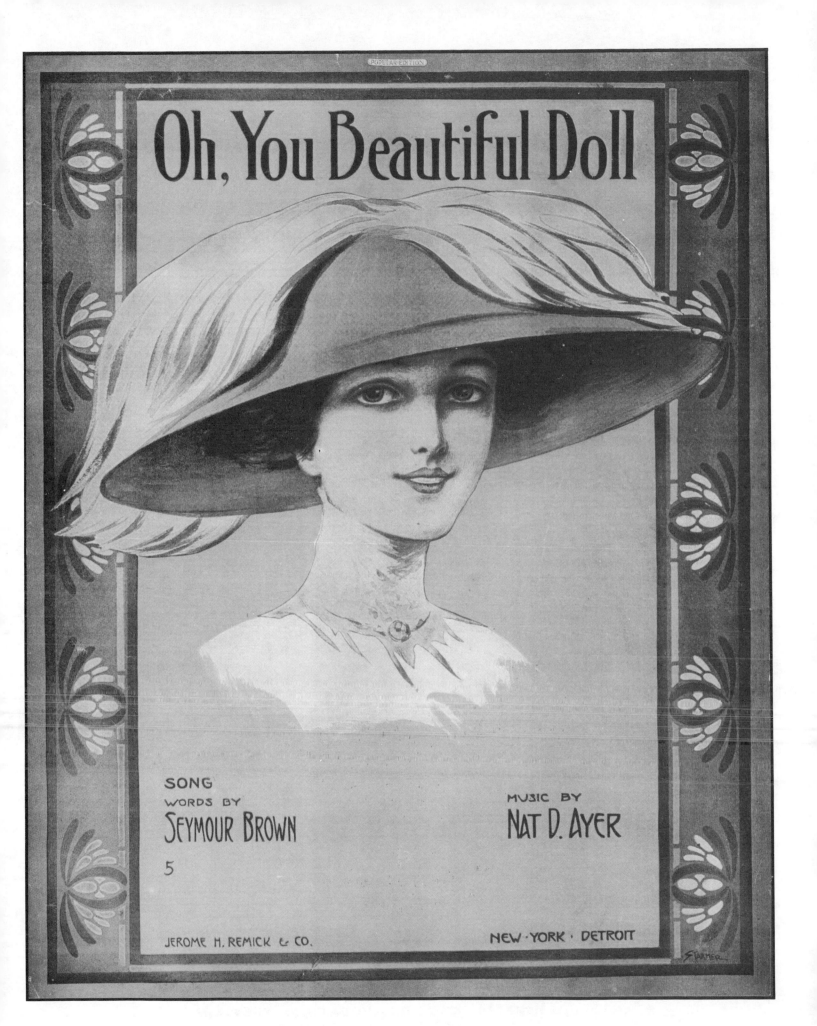

Oh You Beautiful Doll

Words by
A. SEYMOUR BROWN

Music by
NAT. D. AYER

Up to my side,_____ My heart's__ a
A - gain to mine,_____ For love____ is

fire_____ With love's de - sire.
king_____ Of ev'- ry thing.

In my arms, rest com - plete, I nev- er thought that life could ev - er
Squeeze me, dear, I don't care! Hug me just as if you were a

be so sweet Till I met you,_____ some time a go,
griz-zly bear__ This is how_____ I'll go through life,

Oh You Beautiful Doll _4_

But now you know_____ I love you so.
No care or strife_____ When you're my wife.

REFRAIN

Oh!_____ you beau-ti-ful doll, you great, big beau-ti-ful doll!

_____ Let_____ me put my arms a-bout you,

I_____ could nev-er live with-out you; Oh!_____ you

Oh You Beautiful Doll 4

36

beau-ti-ful doll, You great, big beau-ti-ful doll!___ If you ev - er leave_ me how my heart will ache,_ I want to hug_ you but I fear you'd break. Oh, oh, oh, oh, Oh, you beau-ti-ful doll! doll!

ARE WE TO PART LIKE THIS?

by Harry Castling and
Charles Collins

40

"IF THOSE LIPS COULD ONLY SPEAK!"

Written and Composed
by
CHAS. RIDGWELL
and WILL GODWIN.

SUNG IN
the Successful DRAMA
OF THE SAME NAME
being Presented by

MISS DOT STEPHENS'

Specially Selected Company.

6 D net.

London: FRANCIS, DAY & HUNTER LTD
138–140, CHARING CROSS ROAD, W.C.2.
NEW YORK AGENTS: LEO FEIST, Inc., 56, COOPER SQUARE.
SYDNEY AGENTS: J. ALBERT & SON, 137-139, KING STREET.
PAR'S AGENTS: PUBLICATIONS. FRANCIS-DAY S.A., 30, RUE DE L'ECHQUIER.
BERLIN AGENTS: FRANCIS DAY & HUNTER G.m.b.H. LEIPZIGER STR 37, W.8

PRINTED IN ENGLAND.

If Those Lips Could Only Speak!

Sung by WILL GODWIN

Words and Music by
CHAS. RIDGEWELL
and WILL GODWIN

1 He stood in a beau-ti-ful man-sion
2 With all his great pow'r and his rich-es
3 He sat there and gazed at the paint-ing,

Sur-round-ed by rich-es un-told;_____ He gazed at a beau-ti-ful
He knows he can nev-er re-place_____ One thing in the man-sion that's
Then slum-bered for-get-ting all pain,_____ And there in that man-sion in

pic-ture_____ That hung in a frame of gold._____ 'Twas a
ab-sent_____ His wife's ten-der smil-ing face._____ And each
fan-cy,_____ She stood by his side a-gain._____ Then his

F. & D. Ltd. 23115

pic - ture   of   a   la - dy _____   So   beau - ti - ful,
time   he   sees   her   pic - ture _____   These   same   words   you'll
lips   they   soft - ly   mur - mured _____   The   name   of   his

Dm   B♭   A7   B♭

young   and   fair _____   To   the   beau - ti - ful   life -   like
hear   him   say; _____   "All   my   wealth   I   would   free -   ly
once   sweet   bride; _____   With   his   eyes   fixed   up - on   the

Dm   G

fea - tures   He   mur - mured   in   sad   des - pair. _____
for - feit   And   toil   for   you   night   and   day. _____
pic - ture   He   a - woke   from   his   dream   and   cried. _____

C   C°   C   G7   C7

CHORUS

"If   those   lips   could   on - ly   speak _____   If   those   eyes   could   on - ly

p - f

F   D°

F. & D. Ltd. 23115

GLOW WORM

Words by
LILLA CAYLEY ROBINSON

Music by
PAUL LINCKE

lose their way, ___ lest they should lose their way, ___ the glow-worms night - ly ___
by your leave, ___ this se - cret, by your leave, ___ is worth the learn - ing!

Light their ti - ny lan-terns gay, ___ their ti-ny lan-terns gay ___ and twin-kle
When true lov-ers come at eve, ___ true lov-ers come at eve, ___ their hearts are

bright - ly. Here and there, and ev-'ry-where, from mos-sy dell and
burn - ing! Glow-ing cheeks and lips be-tray, how sweet the kis - ses

hol - low, Float-ing, glid-ing through the air, they call on us to
tast - ed! Till we steal the fire a - way, for fear lest it be

fol - low!
wast - ed!"

Shine, lit-tle glow-worm, glim - mer,

shine, lit-tle glow-worm, glim - mer! Lead us, lest too

far we wan - der, Love's sweet voice is call - ing yon - der!

Shine, lit-tle glow-worm, glim - mer, shine, lit-tle glow-worm,

glim - mer! Light the path, be - low, a - bove, and

lead us on to Love! Shine, lit-tle glow-worm, glim - mer,

Ah shine, lit-tle glow-worm, glim - mer, Ah Lead us, lest too

Chorus *ad lib.*

rit. *a tempo* *stacc.*

51

far we wan - der, Love's sweet voice is call - ing yon - der!

Ah

Shine, lit - tle glow - worm, glim - mer, shine, lit - tle glow - worm,

Ah

glim - mer! Light the path, be - low, a - bove, and lead us on to

1. 2.

D. S.

Love! Love!

Die Lustige Witwe.
known as
THE MERRY WIDOW
WALTZES.

by Franz Lehar.
Arr. by Rudolf Thaler.

Introduction.
Allegretto.

VALSE.

1

The M W Waltzes. 8.

Valse lento.

a tempo.

rit.

rit.

pp

f

1

2

The M W Waltzes. 8.

The M W Waltzes. 8.

Finale.

ALEXANDER'S RAGTIME BAND

Words and Music
By IRVING BERLIN

land,............ They can play a bu–gle call like you nev–er heard be-fore, So nat–ur–al that you want to go to war; That's just the best - est band what am, hon–ey lamb, Come on a– long,............... Come on a - long,............... Let me take you by the

hand,........ Up to the man,........ Up to the man............ who's the lead-er of the

band,.............. And if you care to hear the Swa-nee Riv-er played in

rag - time,...... Come on and hear,.............. Come on and hear................. Al - ex-

an - der's rag - time band................. Come on and, band...............

"SOMEWHERE A VOICE IS CALLING"

SONG

Words:

Eileen Newton

Music:

ARTHUR F. TATE

No. 1 in D   No. 2 in E♭   No. 3 in F   No. 4 in G

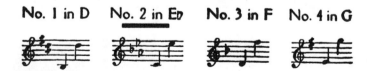

Price **2/-** net
VIOLIN and CELLO OBB.
ALL KEYS - each 6d. net

The Melody of the Song arranged for MILITARY and BRASS Bands.
Published by Messrs. BOOSEY & Co.

The following are the published arrangements of the Song and Melody.

WALTZ (for Piano)	..	2/- net
Full Orchestra	...	1/6 ,,
Small ,,	...	1/- ,,
Extra Parts each		3d. ,,

The Waltz for MILITARY and BRASS Bands published by Messrs. BOOSEY & Co.

		Net.
DUET (High and Low Voices, in G)	...	2/-
DUET (Mezzo and Low Voices, in F)	...	2/-
DUET (Soprano and Tenor, in G)	...	2/-
TRIO (Tenor, Baritone and Bass)	...	2/-
TRIO (Soprano, 1st and 2nd Contralto)	...	2/-
PIANO SOLO	...	2/-
VIOLIN and PIANO	...	2/-
Arranged by William Henley.		
VIOLONCELLO and PIANO ...	...	2/-
Arranged by William Henley.		
CORNET SOLO with ORCHESTRAL ACCOMPT. in F or G	...	1/6
ORCHESTRAL ACCOMPT. for VOICE in D, E♭, F or G	... each	1/6

REPRINTED AND PUBLISHED BY
T. B. HARMS & FRANCIS, DAY & HUNTER, Inc., 62-64, West 45th Street, New York,
By arrangement with **J. H. LARWAY,** Music Publisher, London. **Owner of Copyright.**

"SOMEWHERE A VOICE IS CALLING."

WORDS BY
EILEEN NEWTON.

MUSIC BY
ARTHUR F. TATE.

Slowly and with expression.

con sordini.

Dusk,   and the sha _ dows

fall _ ing _____ O'er   land   and   sea;

L. 1362.

Night, and the stars are gleam - ing — Ten - der and true;

Dear - est my heart is dream - ing, Dream - - ing of you!

Slowly and with intense expression.

Night, and the stars are gleam _ ing, Ten _ der and true;

Dear _ est! my heart is dream _ _ ing,___ Dream _ ing, of

you.___

con sordini.

MUSIC HALL

MARCH MEDLEY

No. 300.

Feldman's 6D *Edition*

This Song may be Sung in Public without Fee or Licence Except at Theatres & Music Halls.

I DO LIKE TO BE BESIDE THE SEASIDE

Written and Composed
by
John H. Glover-Kind.

Sung by
MARK SHERIDAN.

London
B. FELDMAN & CO
2 & 3, ARTHUR STREET, NEW OXFORD STREET, W.C.

6D STRICTLY NETT

MELBOURNE:
176 & 178, COLLINS STREET.

I DO LIKE TO BE BESIDE THE SEASIDE

Written and Composed by

JOHN A. GLOVER-KIND

1. Ev-er-y-one de-
2. Tim-o-thy went to
3. Wil-liam Sykes the

-lights to spend their sum-mer's hol-i-day____ Down be-side the side of the sil-ver-y
{Black-pool
{Bright-on} for the day last Eas-ter-tide____ To see what he could see by the side of the
bur-glar, he'd been out to work one night____ Filled his bag with jew-els cash and

I'm no ex-cept-ion to the rule, in fact, if I'd my
Soon as he reach'd the sta-tion there, the first thing he es-
Con-sta-ble Brown felt quite surprised when Will-iam hove in

marcato il basso

way___ I'd re-side by the side of the sil-ver-y sea.___ But
-pied___ Was the Wine Lodge door, stood o-pen in-vi-ting-ly.___ To
sight___ Said he "The hours you're keeping are far too late"___ So he

sfz

when you're just the common or gar-den Smith or Jones or Brown___ At
quench his thirst, he tod-dled in-side, and called out for a "wine,"___ Which
grabbed him by the col-lar and lodged him safe and sound in jail___ Next

bus-'ness up in town___ You've got to set-tle down___ You
grew to eight or nine___ Till his nose be-gan to shine___ Said
morn-ing look-ing pale___ Bill told a tear-ful tale___ The

save up all the mon-ey you can till sum-mer comes a - round,____ Then a-
he "What peo - ple see in the sea I'm sure I fail to see!"____ So he
judge said, "For a cou-ple of months I'm send-ing you a - way!"____ Said

- way you go To a spot you know, where the cock - le shells are found.
caught the train Back home a - gain, Then to his wife said he!
Bill! "How kind!" Well! If you don't mind Where I spend my hol - i - day,

CHORUS

Oh! I do like to be be-side the sea - side____ I

do like to be be-side the sea____ I do like to

76

stroll up-on the Prom, Prom, Prom, Where the brass - bands play Tid-de-ly -om - pom - pom! So just let me be be-side the sea - side

I'll be be-side my-self with glee And there's lots of girls be-side, I should like to be be - side, Be-side the sea - side!

Be-side the sea! Oh! I sea!

Drum

THE STAR CO'S 6D EDITIONS
Reg. No. 257834.

This Song may be Sung without fee or license except at Theatres and Music Halls.

FALL IN AND FOLLOW ME.

Written by
A. J. Mills

Composed by
Bennett Scott.

SUNG BY

CHAS. R. WHITTLE.

Copyright.

London, W.C.

PRICE 6d NETT.
NO DISCOUNT ALLOWED.

THE STAR MUSIC PUBLISHING CO LTD

51, High Street, New Oxford Street.
(OPPOSITE TOTTENHAM COURT ROAD.)

TELEPHONE 8446 GERRARD.   TELEGRAPHIC ADDRESS, SONGONIA, LONDON.

Copyright MCMX in England and America by The Star Music Publishing Co Ltd.

Fall in and follow Me

Written by
A. J. MILLS.

Composed by
BENNETT SCOTT.

Once he left his quiet su - bur - ban nest,___ With six

pals he went__ up west.___ Said the others, "now what shall we do?___

___ As we want some fun, we'll leave it all to you."___ Then Gib - son

swelled with Mi - li - ta - ry pride,___ Twirling his mous-tache he cried:

CHORUS.

Fall in ___ and follow me! ___ fall in ___ and follow me! ___

Come along and never mind the wea - ther, All to - ge - ther,

stand on me, boys; I know ___ the way to go, ___ I'll take ___

___ you for a spree, ___ You do as I do and you'll do right,

Fall in, ___ and fol-low me! ___ me! ___

81

FALL IN AND FOLLOW ME

Written by A. J. MILLS.   Composed by BENNETT SCOTT.

1.

Mister Gibson, once a Military man,
Uses Military language when he can;
Once he left his quiet suburban nest,
With six pals he went up west.
Said the others, "now what shall we do?
As we want some fun, we'll leave it all to you."
Then Gibson swelled with Military pride,
Twirling his moustache he cried:

CHORUS.

Fall in and follow me! fall in and follow me!
Come along and never mind the weather,
All together, stand on me, boys;
I know the way to go, I'll take you for a spree;
You do as I do and you'll do right,
Fall in, and follow me!

2.

Off they went to see a ballet gay that night,
And the lovely dancing girls gave them delight;
Then behind the scenes they thought they'd go,
Said, "those girls we'd like to know."
Gibson quickly led the way, you're sure,
Through a passage dark until they reached a door;
And then he stopped and whispered low, "I guess
This is where the Fairies dress:"
Chorus — Fall in, and follow me! &c.

3.

Something after twelve they started home again,
Had to walk, they'd lost the last suburban train;
By the old Canal they tramped along,
Singing out the latest song.
Then they saw their wives, oh! what a scream!
Walking up towards them by the flowing stream;
Then Gibson slipped and fell into the tide,
Splashed about and loudly cried:
Chorus — Fall in, and follow me! &c.

No. 109. THE STAR CO'S 6d EDITIONS
Reg. No. 267834.

This Song may be Sung without fee or license except at Theatres and Music Halls.

SHIP AHOY!
(ALL THE NICE GIRLS LOVE A SAILOR)

Written by
A. J. MILLS

Composed by
BENNETT SCOTT.

SUNG BY
MISS HETTY KING.

Copyright.

London, W.C.
THE STAR MUSIC PUBLISHING CO. LTD.
51, High Street, New Oxford Street.
(OPPOSITE TOTTENHAM COURT ROAD.)
TELEPHONE 8446 GERRARD.   TELEGRAPHIC ADDRESS, SONGONIA, LONDON.

PRICE 6d NETT.
NO DISCOUNT ALLOWED.

Copyright 1909 in the United States of America by The Star Music Publishing Co. Ltd.

"SHIP AHOY!"

(All the nice Girls love a Sailor)

Written by
A. J. MILLS

Composed by
BENNETT SCOTT

cage,___ He smiles at all the pret-ty girls Up-on the land-ing stage.
belles,___ Dress'd up *à la* Sa-lom-e, Col-oured beads and oys-ter shells.
smile;___ And you can trust a sail-or, He's a white man all the while!

CHORUS *Slower*

All the nice girls ___ love a sail-or, ___ All the

nice girls ___ love a tar;___ For there's some-thing ___

___ about a sail-or,___ Well, you know what sail-ors

THE ARCADIANS

SELECTIONS

THE ARCADIANS
Selection

Music by
LIONEL MONCKTON & HOWARD TALBOT

Selected and arranged by
H. M. HIGGS

Allegro vivace FROM OPENING CHORUS- ACT II. (Lionel Monckton)

Tempo di Valse "CHORUS OF WAITRESSES" FROM OPENING CHORUS- ACT III. (Howard Talbot)

Plant your po - sies, rue and ro - ses, Flow'rs of ev - 'ry hue; Pink a-

-za - leas, crim - son dah - lias, Li - lac white and blue. See the bare trees, plum and

Copyright, MCMIX, by Chappell & Cº Ltd.
50, New Bond Street, London. W. 1. & Sydney

pear - trees, Bear - ing while you wait; Good to look on, made to hook on,

That's Ar - ca - di - a, Ar - ca - di - a up - to - date!

Tempo di Valse "MY MOTTER" (Howard Talbot)

I've al-ways been, since quite a lad, Chee-ry and gay when things were bad— That is a way I've al - ways

'ad — I look on the bright side! *con 8va ad lib.* I've got-ter mot - ter Al - ways

mer - ry and bright! *con 8va ad lib.* Look a - round and you will find Ev-e-ry cloud is sil - ver-lined; The

sun will shine Al - tho' the sky's a grey one; I've of - ten said to me-

-self, I've said, "Cheer up, cul - ly you'll soon be dead! A short life and a gay one!"

34650

Chappell

Andante "ARCADY IS EVER YOUNG" (Lionel Monckton)

Far away in Ar-ca-dy Summer never pass-es, Warm the wind that wanders free Thro' the bending grass-es; Sunbeams peeping thro' the shade

Mint a gold-en trea-sure; Dimpled Youth goes down the glade Hand in hand with Plea-sure! Hand in hand with Pleasure.

Land of Love and land of Mirth, Land where peace and joy had birth, There the birds have

ev-er sung: Ar-ca-dy, Ar-ca-dy is al-ways young! Ar-ca-dy! Ar-ca-dy! Ah!

SHINE ON, HARVEST MOON

SONG
BY
NORA BAYES and
JACK NORWORTH

Sung by
NORA BAYES and JACK NORWORTH
in
"The Follies of 1908"

JEROME H. REMICK & CO.
NEW YORK   DETROIT

Shine On, Harvest Moon

Words by
JACK NORWORTH

Music by
NORA BAYES - NORWORTH

Moderato.

Night was might – y dark so   you could
I   can't see why the boy should sigh, when

hard – ly   see,   For the moon re – fused to   shine,
by   his   side   is   the girl he loves so   true,

Cou - ple sit - ting un - der - neath a wil - low tree, For love they
All he has to say is "Won't you be my bride, For I love

pine,___ Lit - tle maid was kind a - fraid of dark - ness So she
you,___ Why should I be tell - ing you this se - cret When I

said,_____ "I guess I'll go," Boy be - gan to sigh,
know_____ that you can guess," Har - vest moon will smile,

Looked up at the sky, Told the moon his lit - tle tale of woe.___
Shine on all the while, If the lit - tle girl should an - swer "Yes."___

Shine on harvest moon 3

93

CHORUS.

Oh, shine on, har-vest moon, up in _____ the sky. _____

I _____ ain't had no lov- in' Since A-pril, Jan-u-a-ry, June or Ju - ly,—

Snow time ain't no time to stay _____ out doors and spoon, _____ So,

shine on, shine on, har-vest moon, For me and my gal. _____

Shine on harvest moon 3

94

THAT MESMERIZING MENDELSSOHN TUNE.

Words and Music by

IRVING BERLIN.

Hon - ey, list - en to that dream - y
Don't you stand there, hon - ey, can't you

tune they're play - in', Won't you tell me how on earth you keep from sway - in'?
hear me sigh - in'? Is you gwine to wait un - til I'm al - most dy - in'?

Umm! Umm!   Oh, that Men-dels-sohn   Spring   Song
Umm! Umm!   Oh, that Men-dels-sohn   Spring   Song

tune;   If you ev-er loved me show me now or nev-er,
tune;   Get your-self ac-quaint-ed with some real live woo-in',

Lor' I wish they'd play that mu-sic on for ev-er, Umm! Umm!
Make some fun-ny nois-es like there's some-thing do-in', Umm! Umm!

Oh, that Men-dels-sohn   tune._____ My hon-ey,
Oh, that Men-dels-sohn   tune._____ My hon-ey,

That mesmerizing Mendelssohn tune.

97

CHORUS.
Expressive and legato.

Love ___ me to that ev - er - lov - in' Spring Song me - lo - dy,

Please me, hon-ey, squeeze me to that Mendelssohn strain, Kiss me like you would your mother,

One good kiss de - serves an - oth - er, That ___ the on - ly mu - sic that was

ev - er meant for me, That tan - ta - liz - in', hyp - no - tiz - in',

mesmer - iz - in' Mendelssohn tune. ___ tune. ___

That mesmerizing Mendelssohn tune.
98

DESTINY.

WALTZ.

Composed by
SYDNEY BAYNES.

PIANO.

W. W. & Co Ltd 148.

100

To Orch: ⊕ Coda.

W. W. & Cº Ltd 148.

CODA.

"Waiting For The Robert E Lee"

Words by
L. WOLFE GILBERT

Music by
LEWIS F. MUIR

Allegro moderato

down on the lev - ee in old Al - ab - am - y There's
whis - tles are blow - in' the smoke - stacks are show - in' The

dad - dy and mam - my there's Eph - riam and Sam - my, On a
ropes they are throw - in' ex - cuse me, I'm go - in' To the

Way
The

Waiting For The Robert E Lee

107

Rob - ert E. Lee__that's come To car - ry the cot-ton a - way.____
here comes my ba - by On the good old Rob-ert E Lee.____

Chorus, *p-f*

Watch them shuff - lin' a - long _____ See them shuff-

- lin' a - long _____ Go take your best gal

real pal, Go down to the lev - ee, I said to the lev-

Waiting For The Robert E Lee

-ee-- and   Join that shuff - lin'   throng,_____

Hear that mu - sic and song._____ It's sim - ply great,

mate,   Wait - in' on the lev - ee,   Wait - in' for the

1.
Rob - ert E. Lee._____

2.
Lee._____

D.S.

Waiting For The Robert E Lee

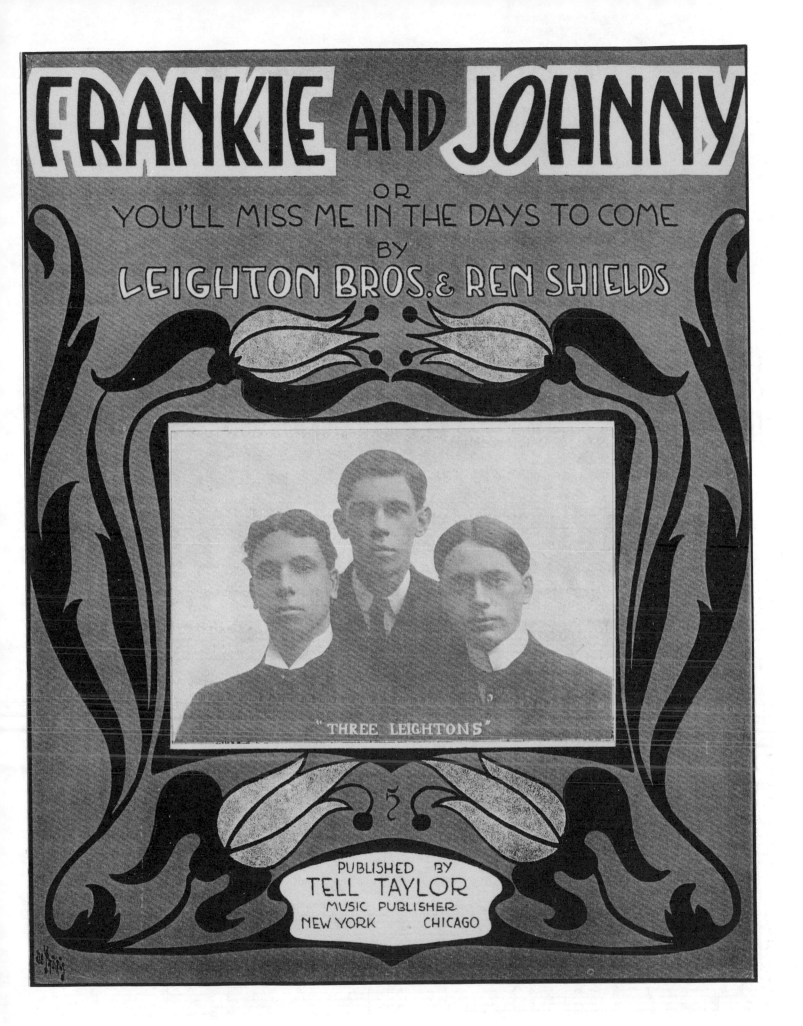

"THREE LEIGHTONS"

FRANKIE AND JOHNNY

or
"You'll Miss Me In The Days To Come"

LEIGHTON BROS.
&
REN SHIELDS.

Frank-ie and John-ny were sweet-hearts   They had a quar-rel one
Frank-ie says "lis-ten now John-ny___   To prove my love is
Frank-ie then said to her John-ny___   "Say man your hour has
"Send for your rub-ber tired hears-es ___   Go get your rub-ber tired

day,   John-ny he vowed that he would leave her___
true,"   Ev-er-y dol-lar I can save dear___
come,"   From un-der neath her silk ki-mon-a ___
hacks,   Take lov-in John-ny to the grave-yard

Copyright 1912 by Tell Taylor. Chicago, Ill.

Said he was go - in' a - way, He's nev-er com-in' home, _____ _____ He's goin' a-way to roam _____ Frank-ie she begged and plead-ed Cried oh Johnny please stay, _____ She says my hon-ey I have

I'm goin to give _____ to you So I think now dear, _____ _____ That ought to keep you here'' _____ John-ny says "list - en now Frank-ie Don't want to tell you no lie, _____ I've lost my heart to an-

She drew a fort-y-four gun Oh it was a bear, _____ _____ 'Twas quite a large af - fair, _____ Johnny he dashed down the stair-way Cryin' "Oh Frankie don't shoot" _____ Frankie took aim with her

I shot him in _____ the back With my great big gun, _____ _____ Just as he went to run, _____ Send for a thousand po - lice - men De-tect-ives right a - way _____ Lock me way down in the

Frankie & Johnny, 4

113

done you wrong, But please don't go_____ a - way Then John-ny
o - ther queen, Her name is Nel - lie Bly" Then Frank-ie
"For-ty - four" Five times with a root-y-toot-toot As John-ny
dun-geon cell And throw the keys_____ a - way My John-ny's

sighed, _____ and to his Frank-ie cried. _____
groaned, _____ as her John-ny moaned. _____
fell, _____ Then Miss Frank-ie yelled. _____
dead, _____ just be-cause he said." _____

REFRAIN.

mf - ff

VERSES

1, 2 & 4. "Oh, I'm a - goin' a - way and I'm a - goin' to stay I'm nev-er
3d Verse. "Oh, you're a - goin' a - way and you're a - goin' to stay you're nev-er

mf - ff

com - in' home _____ You're goin' to miss me hon', in the
com - in' home _____ I'm goin' to miss you hon', in the

Frankie & Johnny. 4

days to come, When the win-ter winds begin to blow The ground is covered up with snow You'll
days to come When the win-ter winds begin to blow The ground is covered up with snow I'll

think of me and you will wish to be Back with your
think of thee and I will wish to be Back with my

lov - in' man. _____ You're go-in' to miss me hon', in the
lov - in' man. _____ I'm go-in' to miss you hon', in the

days, days, days to come. _____ Oh, I'm a - ___
days, days, days to come. _____ Oh, you're a - ___

"SILVER HEELS."

Melody taken from the popular Indian Intermezzo.

Writers of the tremendous successes,
"HIAWATHA" "MOONLIGHT" etc.

Poem by JAMES O'DEA.

Music by NEIL MORET.

Not too fast.

Where the
When the

Moderato.

corn - flow'rs wave once an In - dian brave, All un - fet - tered by the white man's
sum - mer goes and the north - wind blows, In a co - zy lit - tle wig - wam

law,   Loved a pret - ty lit - tle crow - foot squaw   Just the
we,   "Will be al - ways right at home" said he   "With a

sweet-est and the neat-est lit-tle girl he ev-er saw. She was
hub-by and a chub-by lit-tle pa-poose on your knee." But the

al-ways coy to this In-dian boy, To his heart she did-n't do a
maid-en shy on-ly dropped her eye, As a ten-der lit-tle sigh she

thing When the moon beams on the riv-er set the
sighed While her cop-per col-ored lov-er 'neath the

rall.

sha-dows all a-qui-ver, then he'd sing:
sil-v'ry stars a-bove her, once more cried:

rall.

I love you and you love me, Pret-ty lit tle Sil - ver Heels

I'll build you a big tee-pee, If you will come and cook my meals

Young Chief's blue and all for you, Plen-ty heap he love sick feels

Don't be miss-ing, heap much kiss-ing, Sil - ver Heels.

SILVER HEELS

I love you and you love me, Pret-ty lit-tle Sil-ver Heels

I'll build you a big tee-pee, If you will come and cook my meals

Young Chief's blue and all for you, Plen-ty heap he love sick feels

Don't be miss-ing, heap much kiss-ing, Sil-ver Heels.

SILVER HEELS

119

SILVERHEELS
INDIAN INTERMEZZO - TWO STEP

BY - NEIL MORET
COMPOSER OF
'HIAWATHA' 'MOONLIGHT'
PUBLISHED BY
JEROME H. REMICK & CO
NEW YORK — DETROIT

Dedicated to EUGENE STRATTON.

THE LILT OF LAGUNA

Barn Dance and Cake Walk

Founded on LESLIE STUARTS Popular Songs.

By KARL KAPS.

Price, .. 4/=
Band Parts, 1/=nett.

LONDON;
FRANCIS, DAY & HUNTER, 142 CHARING CROSS ROAD, (OXFORD STREET END.)
Publishers of, Smallwood's Celebrated Pianoforte Tutor. Smallwood's 55 Melodious Exercises, Etc .
NEW YORK: T. B. HARMS & Cº 18 EAST 22ND STREET.
Copyright MDCCCXCIX in the United States of America, by Francis, Day & Hunter.
H.G.BANKS, Lith.

Telegraphic Address.
ARPEGGIO LONDON

LILY OF LAGUNA

Sung by EUGENE STRATTON

Written & Composed by

LESLIE STUART

1. It's de same old tale of a pal-pa-ting nig-gar ev-'ry
2. When I first met Lil it was down in old La-gu-na at de

time, ev-'ry time; It's de same old
dance, od-er night; So she says, "Say, a'm

trou-ble of a coon Dat wants to be mar-ried ve-ry soon; It's de
cu-rious for to know When ye leave here de way yer goin' to go, 'Kase a

same old heart dat is long-ing for it's la-dy ev-'ry time, yes ev-'ry
wants to see who de la-dy is dat claims ye all way home, way home to-

time, But not de same gal, not de same gal,__ She is ma
-night." I says,"I've no gal, nev-er had one!"__ And den ma

Lil-y, ma Lil-y, ma Lil-y gal! She goes ev-'ry
Lil-y, ma Lil-y, ma Lil-y gal! She says, Kern't be-

sun-down,__ yes, ev-'ry sun-down call-in' in de cat-tle up de moun-tain;
-lieve ye,__ a kern't be-lieve ye, else I'd like to have ye shap-per-oon me;

I go 'kase she wants me,___ yes,'kase she wants me help her do de
Dad says he'll es-scortch me,___ says he'll es-scortch me, But it's migh-ty

call-in' and de count-in'. She plays her mu-sic___ to call de
ea-sy for to lose him." Since then each sun down___ I wan-der

lone lambs___ dat roam a-bove,___ But I'm de black sheep and I'm
down here___ and roam a-round___ Un-til I know ma la-dy

wait-in' For de sig-nal of ma lit-tle la-dy love.
wants me, Till I hear de mu-sic ob de sig-nal sound.

124

CHORUS

She's ma la - dy love,___ she is ma dove, ma ba - by love,

She's no gal for sit - tin' down to dream, She's de on - ly queen La -

- gu - na knows; I know she likes me, I know she

likes me Bo-kase she says so; She is de Lil - y of La -

- gu - na, she is my Lil-y and my Rose. Rose.

D.C

OUR MISS GIBBS.
Selection.

Music by
IVAN CARYLL & LIONEL MONCKTON.

Selected and arranged by
H. M. HIGGS.

SONGE D'AUTOMNE.
(Dream of Autumn.)

VALSE.

By ARCHIBALD JOYCE.
Composer of
Vision of Salome Valse. etc.

INTRODUCTION.
Andante moderato.

PIANO.

Tempo di Valse.

129

To Orch: Coda.

P. & D. 10517.

CODA.

Orch: Coda.

F. & D. 10517.

Printed by HENDERSON & SPALDING, Ltd., Sylvan Grove, Old Kent Road, London, S. E. 15.

Raggin' the Waves

By Harry Poole

Arr. Linda M. Cummings

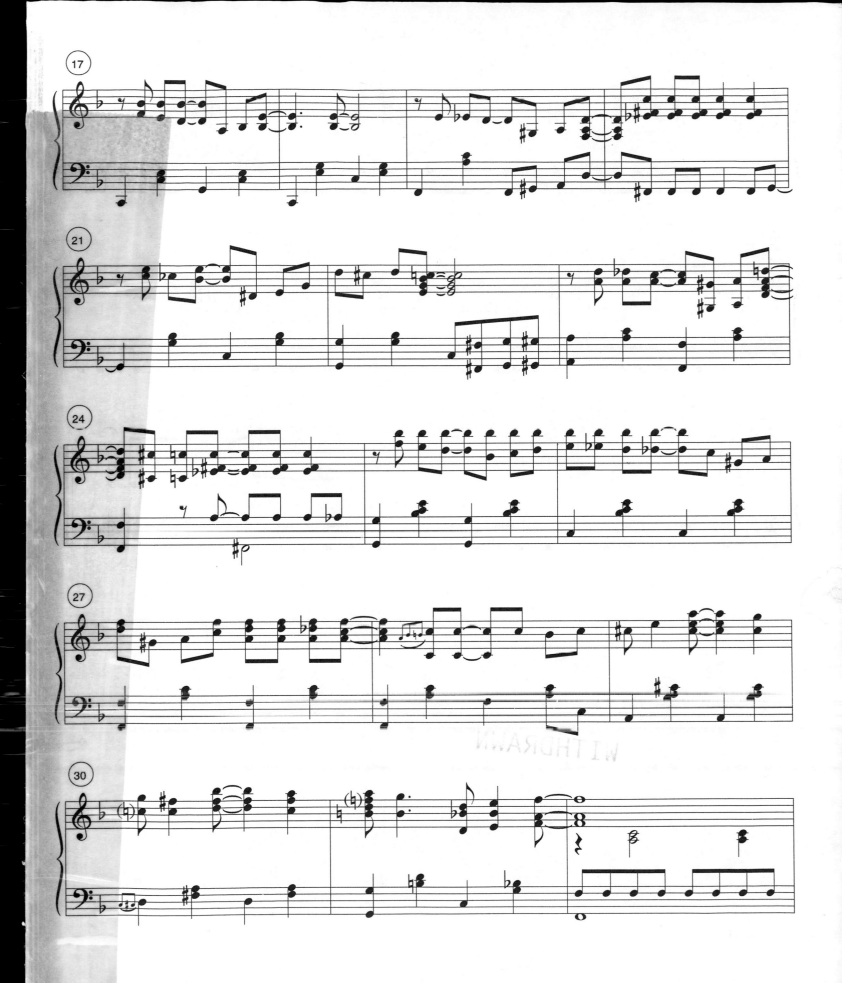

WITHDRAWN